My ENGLISH Sticker Atlas

Catherine Bruzzone and Louise Millar

Illustrations by Stu McLellan

Contents

b small publishing
www.bsmall.co.uk

مرحبا 你好

Using this atlas

This atlas will show you how important languages are in our world. The world is huge but we now have the chance to meet and speak to people from many other countries. Of course we can't speak every language in the world but we can be curious and interested and prepared to learn a few words and phrases. Language is the key to making new friends.

This atlas has maps of the following regions:

On pages 18 and 19 all the countries are listed region by region according to their number on the maps so you can find them more easily. On page 20 are useful map words for you to try and find. On the inside back cover are the answers to questions about the languages of the different regions.

Using the stickers

Each sticker has a caption to help you find where it fits. The stickers will show you some of the important food, animals, plants, industries, natural features, crops and monuments in each region.

नमस्ते สวัสดี

γεια σου שלום

Languages of the world

How many languages do you know? There are thousands of languages in the world and many different alphabets (you can see just a few around the border of this page). The island of Papua New Guinea (see page 14) has over 700! And most people in the world are bilingual, they speak more than one language.

You will find lists of the official or national languages of the countries shown on these maps. The national language is the language used by the government, in education, media and work. Not everyone can speak the national language in their country.

The eight main national languages in the world are: English, Mandarin Chinese, Hindi, Spanish, Russian, French, Arabic and Portuguese. English is used in the most countries but Mandarin Chinese is spoken by the most people.

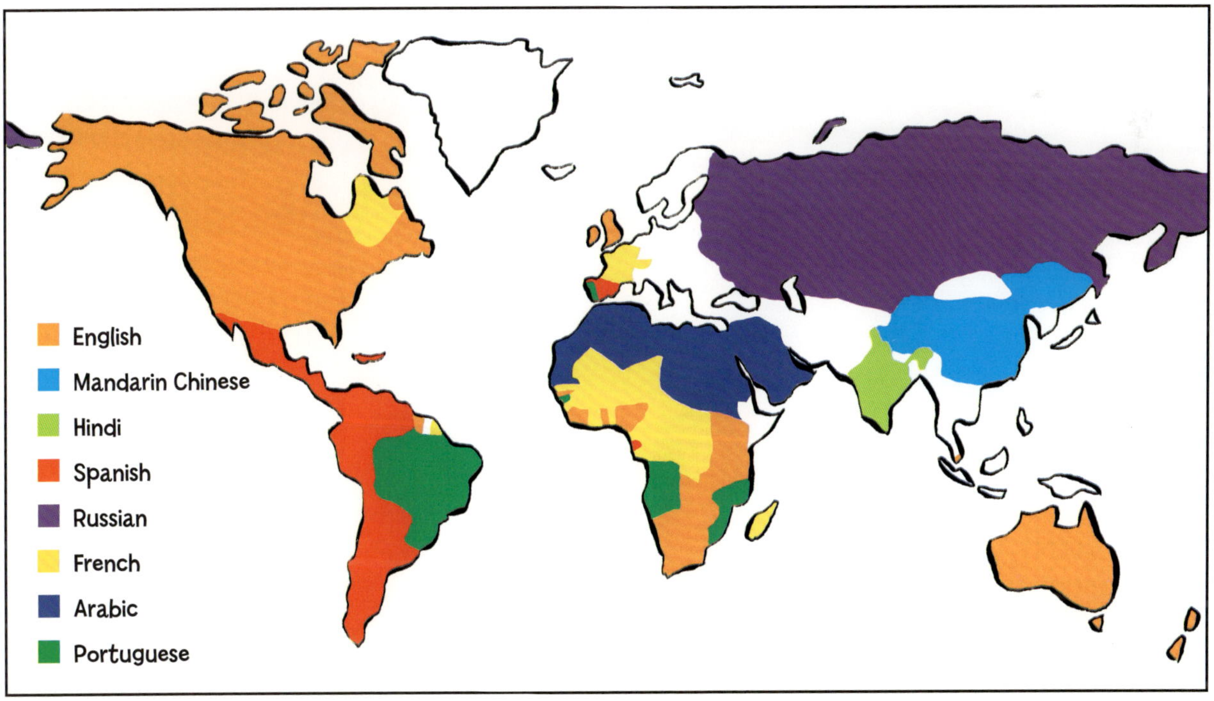

здравствуй

North and Central America

National languages of North and Central America

There are only three national languages spoken in the countries on this map: English, French and Spanish. Do you know which are the countries where these languages are spoken? Answers on inside back cover.

Find the stickers from the centre of the book to match these words.

fruit

bear

cactus

computers

canyon

wheat

Statue of Liberty

South America

National languages of South America
There are five national languages spoken in the countries on this map: Dutch, English, French, Spanish and Portuguese.

Most of the countries in South America speak one language? Which one? Where are the other languages spoken? Answers on inside back cover.

Find the stickers from the centre of the book to match these words.

oil

coffee

orchid

rainforest

cathedral

beef

llama

Europe

1 ICELAND
ARCTIC OCEAN
2 NORWAY
ATLANTIC OCEAN
3 SWEDEN
4 DENMARK
BALTIC SEA
6 RUS
NORTH SEA
36 IRELAND
37 UNITED KINGDOM
London
Thames River
Berlin
28 POLAND
38 NETHERLANDS
Rhine River
41 GERMANY
39 BELGIUM
40 LUXEMBOURG
29 CZECH REPUBLIC
Paris
30 AUSTRIA
27 SLOVAKIA
35 FRANCE
42 SWITZERLAND
ALPS
26 HUNGARY
BAY OF BISCAY
Rhone River
25 SLOVENIA
24 CROATIA
22 BOSNIA & HERZEGOVINA
Po River
31 ITALY
PYRENEES
Corsica (France)
Rome
21 MONTENEGRO
18 ALBANIA
Madrid
Tagus River
34 PORTUGAL
33 SPAIN
Balearic Islands (Spain)
Sardinia (Italy)
MEDITERRANEAN SEA
17 GREEC
Sicily (Italy)
32 MALTA

National languages of Europe

There are 37 national languages spoken in the countries on this map:

Albanian	German	Montenegrin
Belarusian	Greek	Norwegian
Bosnian	Hungarian	Polish
Bulgarian	Icelandic	Portuguese
Croatian	Irish	Romanian
Czech	Italian	Russian
Danish	Latvian	Serbian
Dutch	Lithuanian	Slovak
English	Luxembourgish	Slovenian
Estonian	Macedonian	Spanish
Finnish	Maltese	Swedish
French	Moldovan	Turkish
		Ukrainian

Can you find the countries on the map?

French and German are spoken in several countries. Do you know which?

Answers on inside back cover.

Find the stickers from the centre of the book to match these words.

cheese

sheep

pine tree

cars

tomatoes

river

castle

Africa

MEDITERRANEAN SEA
1 MOROCCO
2 TUNISIA
3 ALGERIA
4 LIBYA
5 EGYPT
Cairo
Canary Islands (Spain)
6 WESTERN SAHARA
Sahara Desert
RED SEA
Tropic of Cancer
7 MAURITANIA
21 NIGER
22 CHAD
23 SUDAN
Nile River
25 ERITREA
26 DJIBOUTI
27 SOMALIA
28 ETHIOPIA
53 CAPE VERDE
8 SENEGAL
9 GAMBIA
10 GUINEA BISSAU
11 MALI
12 GUINEA
13 BURKINA FASO
Niger River
19 BENIN
20 NIGERIA
14 SIERRA LEONE
15 IVORY COAST
17 GHANA
18 TOGO
16 LIBERIA
Lagos
29 CENTRAL AFRICAN REPUBLIC
24 SOUTH SUDAN
30 CAMEROON
31 EQUATORIAL GUINEA
32 SÃO TOMÉ AND PRÍNCIPE
35 GABON
36 REPUBLIC OF CONGO
Congo River
Equator
33 UGANDA
Lake Victoria
34 KENYA
Mount Kenya
Nairobi
37 RWANDA
38 BURUNDI
Mount Kilimanjaro
39 DEMOCRATIC REPUBLIC OF
40 TANZANIA
INDIAN OCEAN
55 SEYCHELLES

Food

North and Central America pages 4-5

fruit

South America pages 6-7

beef

Africa pages 10-11

cocoa chocolate

Europe pages 8-9

cheese

Asia pages 12-13

rice

Australia, New Zealand and the Pacific Islands pages 14-15

butter

The Arctic Ocean page 17

goose

Animals

Africa pages 10-11

elephant

Europe pages 8-9

sheep

Antarctica page 16

penguin

North and Central America pages 4-5

bear

South America pages 6-7

llama

Asia pages 12-13

tiger

Australia, New Zealand and the Pacific Islands pages 14-15

kangaroo

The Arctic Ocean page 17

polar bear

Put the gold stars on the countries you have been to, the country you live in now and the country (or countries) your family comes from. Put purple stars on the countries you would like to visit.

Monuments

Asia pages 12-13

Great Wall

Australia, New Zealand and the Pacific Islands pages 14-15

Sydney Harbour Bridge

South America pages 6-7

cathedral

North and Central America pages 4-5

Statue of Liberty

Europe pages 8-9

castle

Antarctica page 16

ice science laboratory

Africa pages 10-11

pyramid

Plants

Africa pages 10-11

palm tree

Asia pages 12-13

bamboo

South America pages 6-7

orchid

North and Central America pages 4-5

cactus

Europe pages 8-9

pine tree

Australia, New Zealand and the Pacific Islands pages 14-15

coconut palm

Antarctica page 16

seaweed

Crops

Africa pages 10-11

maize

Antarctica page 16

fish

North and Central America pages 4-5

wheat

Asia pages 12-13

tea

Australia, New Zealand and the Pacific Islands pages 14-15

sugar cane

South America pages 6-7

coffee

Europe pages 8-9

tomatoes

Industries

Africa pages 10-11

tourist

Europe pages 8-9

cars

Asia pages 12-13

exploring space

North and Central America pages 4-5

computers

Australia, New Zealand and the Pacific Islands pages 14-15

gold mining

Antarctica page 16

science

South America pages 6-7

oil

Natural Features

North and Central America pages 4-5

canyon

Asia pages 12-13

mountain

Australia, New Zealand and the Pacific Islands pages 14-15

desert

South America pages 6-7

rainforest

Africa pages 10-11

jungle

The Arctic Ocean page 17

ice

Europe pages 8-9

river

National languages of Africa

There are 27 national languages spoken on this continent:

Afrikaans	Kirundi	Southern Sotho	Venda
Amharic	Malagasy	Spanish	Xhosa
Arabic	Northern Ndebele	Swahili	Zulu
Chichewa	Northern Sotho	Swati	
Comorian	Portuguese	Tamazight	
English	Sango	Tigrinya	
French	Seychellois Creole	Tsonga	
Kinyarwanda	Somali	Tswana	

What are the national languages of the following three countries: Ivory Coast, Egypt and Kenya? Answers on inside back cover.

Find the stickers from the centre of the book to match these words.

elephant

maize

cocoa/ chocolate

palm tree

jungle

pyramid

tourist

Asia

National languages of Asia

There are 38 national languages spoken in the countries on this map:

Arabic
Armenian
Azerbaijani
Bengali
Burmese
Chinese (Mandarin)
Dari
Dzongkha
English
Farsi (Persian)
Filipino (Tagalog)
Georgian
Hebrew
Hindi
Indonesian
Japanese
Kazakh
Khmer
Korean
Kyrgyz
Lao
Malay
Maldivian
Mongolian
Nepali
Pashtu
Portuguese
Russian
Sinhala
Tajik
Tamil
Tetum
Thai
Turkish
Turkmen
Urdu
Uzbeki
Vietnamese

Russian, Arabic, and Farsi (or Persian) are the national languages in several countries. Do you know which? Answers on inside back cover.

Find the stickers from the centre of the book to match these words.

rice

bamboo

tiger

Great Wall

mountain

tea

exploring space

Australia, New Zealand and the Pacific Islands

National languages of Australia, New Zealand and the Pacific Islands

There are 14 national languages spoken in the countries on this map:

Bislama	French	Nauruan
English	Hiri Motu	Palauan
Fijian	Kiribati	Samoan
Fijian Hindi	Marshallese	Tok Pisin
	Māori	Tongan

Where do you think English is the national language? Answers on inside back cover.

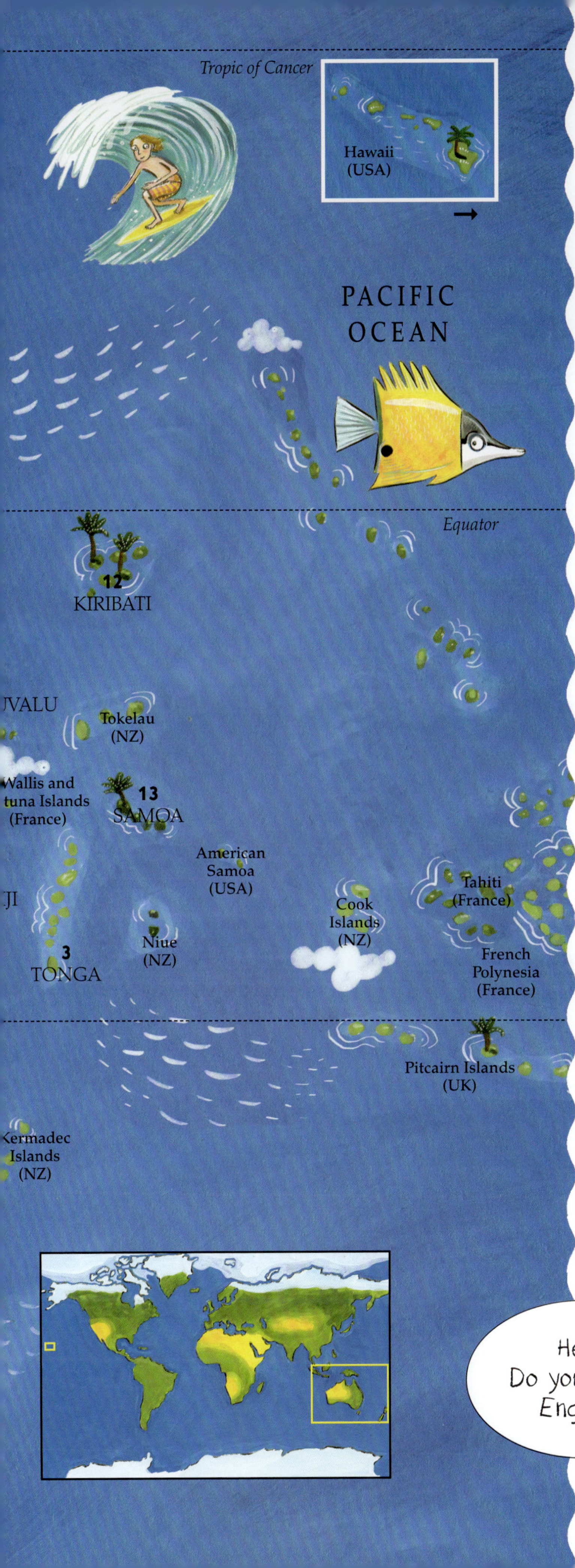

Find the stickers from the centre of the book to match these words.

butter

kangaroo

coconut palm

sugar cane

gold mining

desert

Sydney Harbour Bridge

Antarctica

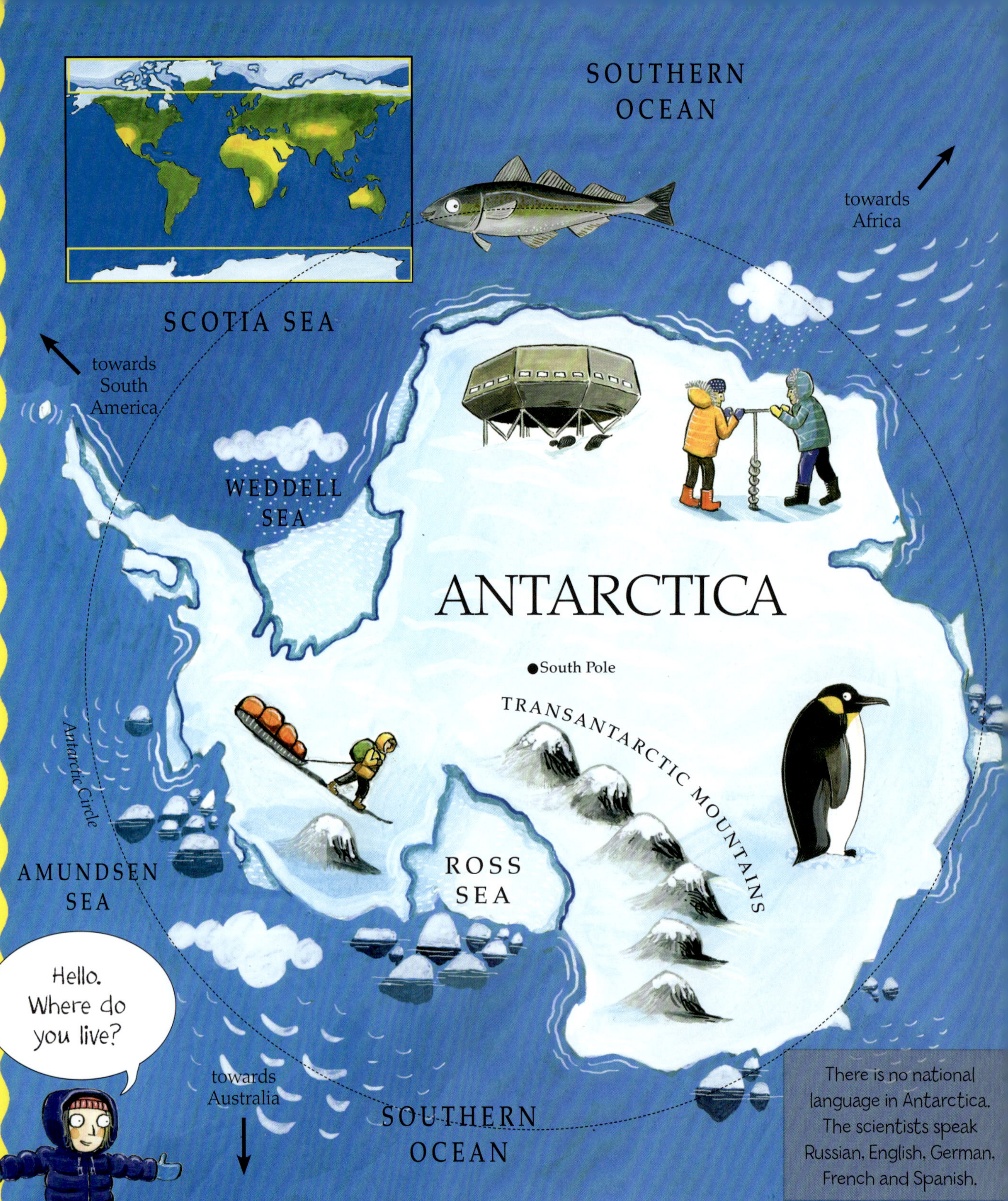

There is no national language in Antarctica. The scientists speak Russian, English, German, French and Spanish.

Find the stickers from the centre of the book to match these words.

fish

penguin

ice science laboratory

science

The Arctic Ocean

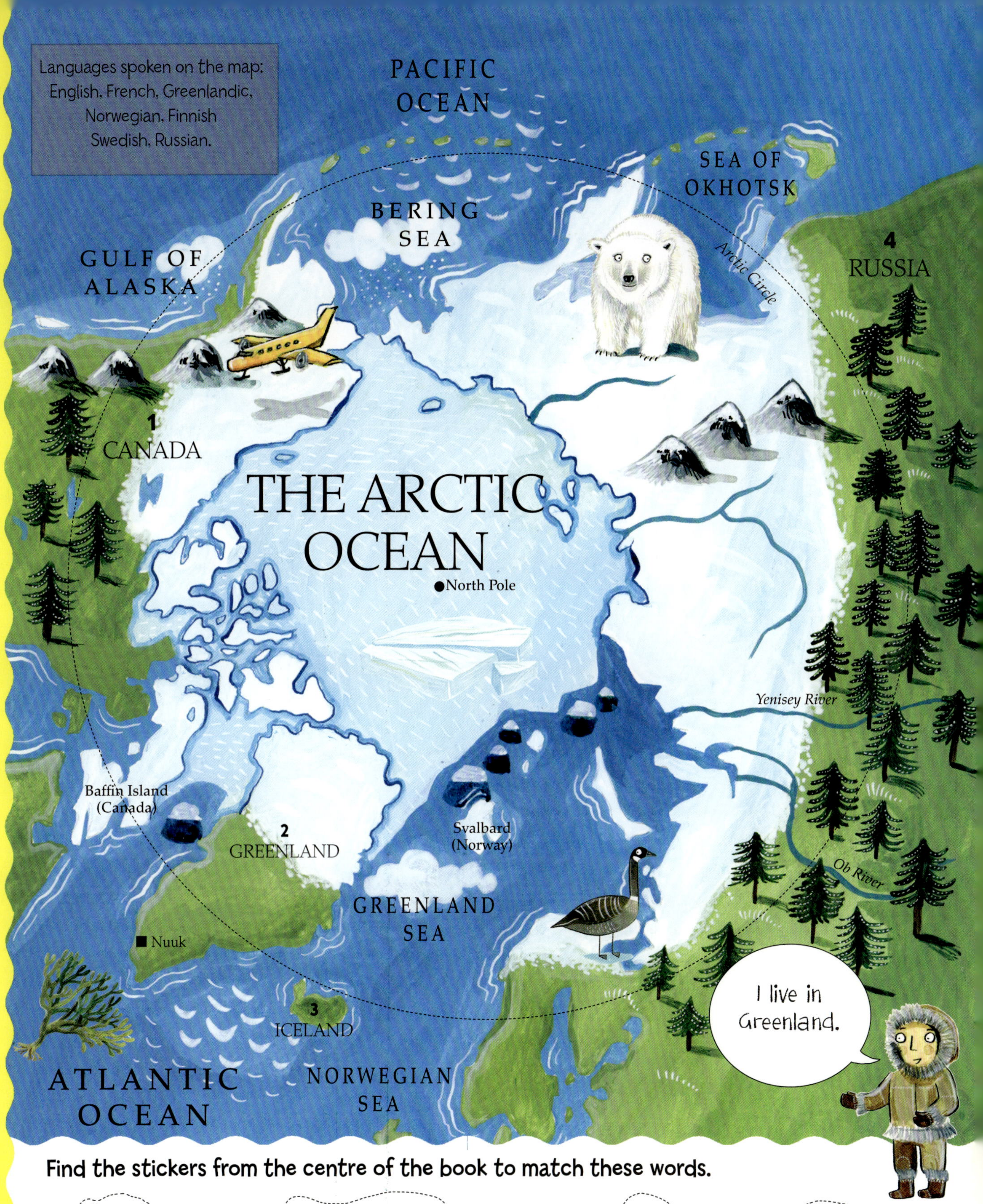

Find the stickers from the centre of the book to match these words.

seaweed

polar bear

goose

ice

Names of countries

North and Central America p.4

1 Canada
2 United States of America
3 Mexico
4 Guatemala
5 Belize
6 Honduras
7 San Salvador
8 Nicaragua
9 Costa Rica
10 Panama
11 The Bahamas
12 Cuba
13 Jamaica
14 **Haiti**
15 Dominican Republic
16 Puerto Rico
17 Leeward Islands
18 Windward Islands
19 Trinidad and Tobago
Alaska (USA)
Hawaii (USA)

South America p.6

1 Colombia
2 Venezuela
3 Guyana
4 Surinam
5 French Guiana
6 Brazil
7 Paraguay
8 Uruguay
9 Argentina
10 Chile
11 Bolivia
12 Peru
13 Ecuador

Europe p.8

1 Iceland
2 Norway
3 Sweden
4 Denmark
5 Finland
6 Russia
7 Estonia
8 Latvia
9 Lithuania
10 Belarus
11 Ukraine
12 Moldova
13 Romania
14 Bulgaria
15 Turkey
16 Cyprus
17 Greece
18 Albania
19 Macedonia
20 Kosovo
21 Montenegro
22 Bosnia & Herzegovina
23 Serbia
24 Croatia
25 Slovenia
26 Hungary
27 Slovakia
28 Poland
29 Czech Republic
30 Austria
31 Italy
32 Malta
33 Spain
34 Portugal
35 France
36 Ireland
37 United Kingdom
38 Netherlands
39 Belgium
40 Luxembourg
41 Germany
42 Switzerland
Balearic Islands (Spain)
Corsica (France)
Sardinia (Italy)
Sicily (Italy)
Crete (Greece)

See if you can find these on the maps:

river
mount
mountain
desert
forest
canyon
falls
lake
island
bay (of)
gulf (of)
sea (of)
ocean
cape

Antarctic Circle
Arctic Circle
Equator
Tropic of Capricorn
Tropic of Cancer

Arctic Ocean
Pacific Ocean
Atlantic Ocean
Indian Ocean
Southern Ocean

Hudson Bay
Gulf of Mexico
Bay of Biscay
Bay of Bengal
Gulf of Alaska
Cape Horn

Caribbean Sea
North Sea
Baltic Sea
Mediterranean Sea
Black Sea
Bering Sea
Sea of Okhotsk
Sea of Japan
South China Sea
Arabian Sea
Red Sea
Caspian Sea
Tasman Sea
Scotia Sea
Weddell Sea
Amundsen Sea
Ross Sea
Greenland Sea
Norwegian Sea

Thames River
Tagus River
Rhone River
Rhine River
Indus River
Yellow River
Yangtze River

USA (United States of America)
UK (United Kingdom)

Rocky Mountains
Andes Mountains
Carpathian Mountains
Alps
Pyrenees
Table Mountain
Mount Kenya
Mount Kilimanjaro
Himalayas
Mount Everest
Great Dividing Range
Southern Alps
Transantarctic Mountains

Grand Canyon
The Great Lakes
Angel Falls
Niagara Falls
Victoria Falls
Lake Victoria
Amazon Rainforest
Great Barrier Reef

Atacama Desert
Sahara Desert
Kalahari Desert
Gobi Desert

South Pole
North Pole

London
Athens
Tehran
Beijing
Cairo